The ABCs

of My
Feelings *and* Music

By

Scott and *Stephanie Edgar*

Illustrated by

Nancy Sosna Bohm

GIA

GIA Publications, Inc.

This book is dedicated to our children: Nathan Edgar,

Layla Bohm, Madeline Bohm, and Chloe Hope Bohm Yonker.

We hope you always seek to find beauty in art and music.

We love you!

The authors have created links to playlists of the repertoire mentioned in this book, and encourage you as a reader to make your own playlists or find alternative versions of the suggested works. To access the playlists, visit giamusic.com/abcs

The ABCs of My Feelings and Music
Scott and Stephanie Edgar
Nancy Sosna Bohm

G-10153

ISBN 978-1-62277-462-3

GIA Publications, Inc.
7404 S. Mason Ave.
Chicago, IL 60638
www.giamusic.com

Layout design by Martha Chlipala
This book was printed in May 2021 by R.R. Donnelley in Dongguan, China

Introduction

Guided by the construct of Social Emotional Learning (SEL), the authors and illustrator of this book sought to provide a resource encouraging a thoughtful connection between music, art, and emotion. The first step to social emotional competence is self-awareness, with the ability to articulate emotions being a hallmark skill in that area. We need to be able to speak about how we are feeling in words beyond "good" and "bad." Music and art can serve as tangible entry points to discussions about artistic aesthetics, emotional intent of the composer/artist, and how art can make us feel, beginning at a very young age. We hope this book helps you and your children/students expand emotional vocabulary, have meaningful discussions about emotions, and think about how music and art makes us feel! The emotions and music we chose are meant to be *possible* examples. There are many other emotions to explore and musical examples evoking them. We also chose to limit the scope of musical examples to Western art music. We acknowledge that this limits the range to one particular genre; however, we valued the ability for each emotion and musical example to be comparable. Jazz, popular, and world musics could also be powerful examples of musical emotion and should be explored. This book is meant to be interactive and inspire dialogue. Listen to each selection, agree, disagree, debate; there is no right or wrong answer. Thank you to Dr. Donald Meyer for his help exploring appropriate repertoire for this work. We hope you enjoy exploring the heart of music!

The Music

Scott Edgar

Music makes us feel many things. It can make us happy or sad, but that is just the beginning. Each letter of the alphabet has an emotion and multiple pieces of music suggested for listening. First, define what the emotion means to you and your children/students. Develop your definition of the emotion and brainstorm about when you have felt this emotion in your lives. Then, listen to the music and decide which piece makes you feel the emotion the most. Think about how fast or slow the music is. What is the tonality? Does the title help us feel the emotion? Did the composer intend a specific emotion to be represented? Were they successful?

A brief historical look at each piece may be beneficial. The music can often emotionally speak for itself. Some of these pieces were chosen because the compositional elements suggested the emotion to us. Others were chosen because of plot (programmatic music), composer intent, or historical context. We have chosen not to suggest which pieces were chosen for what reasons. All of these reasons could be effective in portraying an emotion. It is up to you to decide why a piece of music and emotion are linked! We suggest listening to the music prior to leading a discussion in a classroom setting. Some of the recommended pieces have familiar melodies that guided our decisions; however, they begin later in the piece. The complete pieces are optimal, but the length of some may make them difficult to implement in a class setting. Selecting an excerpt would be completely appropriate. After exploring our suggestions, a great extension would be to find other pieces that could exemplify these emotions. This is just the beginning of developing a robust emotional vocabulary and understanding it through the music. We suggest typing the piece of music (as written in the book) into a search engine or YouTube to find reference recordings. Different performance interpretations of the same piece could also offer nuanced takes on the emotions.

The Art

Nancy Sosna Bohm

In an alphabet book, each letter has a word that serves as a mnemonic device for that letter. Here these words name emotions with images and music in turn, hinting at those emotions and their alphabetical signifiers. Just as handwriting gives clues to the emotions of the writer, the shapes of the fonts and the colors of the letters can also reinforce the meanings of the emotion words, as do the colors of the backgrounds. However, in pictorial representations, colors are chosen for a variety of reasons, including clarity of form and position derived from contrasting colors. Here, the people are painted in shades of blue, purple, and green to avoid racial identification associated with a particular emotion. Just as individuals often express the same emotion differently, there is no one way to depict an emotion. A conversation can develop about what other colors might be used to represent a particular emotion. The background textures were achieved by placing plastic wrap on damp watercolors and allowing them to dry before removing the crinkled plastic— an easy, economical project for young children that might stimulate further conversation about feelings related to colors, perhaps while listening to the musical pieces assigned to the feelings. The body language and facial expressions of the people are intended to more overtly convey the emotions of the assigned words, but discussion might encourage suggestions of other nuances of an emotion or different interpretations entirely. The objects in the images were chosen for their commonality across cultures, but universality should not be assumed; for example, not every child has had an opportunity to see fruit growing on a tree. The ensuing discussion might encourage the children to later engage in interpreting other art with unfamiliar imagery, and to not be afraid to consider the expression of feelings in themselves and others.

Music Discussion Questions for Each Letter

- Define the emotion. When have you felt this way?
- Which piece of music makes you feel the emotion the most?
- Are there other emotions this music makes you feel?
- What elements of the music make you feel the emotion?

   Tonality—major, minor, modal, chromatic, consonant, dissonant?

   Tempo—fast or slow?

   Articulation—short, long, accented?

   Tessitura—high or low sounds?

   Instrumentation?

- Was it the music that made you feel the emotion or another element such as title, historical context, personal experience with the work, or composer intent?

Art Discussion Questions for Each Letter

- How does the picture make you feel?

   Is it a different emotion than the word in the picture?

   What elements of the picture make you feel the emotion?

   Do the colors remind you of this emotion?

   Do the shapes of the letters remind you of this emotion?

- Do the people in the picture seem to feel the same way you feel?
- How would you draw the picture differently to show the emotion?
- Can you think of another emotion that begins with this letter?
- What colors or images might express this emotion?

A: Affection

Léo Delibes: The Flower Duet *from* Lakmé

Sergei Rachmaninov: Symphony No. 2, mvt. 3 (*Adagio*)

Pyotr Tchaikovsky: Love Theme *from* Romeo and Juliet

B: Brave

Ottorino Respighi: Pines of the Appian Way *from* Pines of Rome

Richard Wagner: Ride of the Valkyries *from* Die Walküre

Giuseppe Verdi: Triumphal March *from* Aïda

C: Confused

Charles Ives: The Unanswered Question

Sergei Prokofiev: Symphony No. 2 in D minor, mvt. 1 (*Allegro ben articolato*)

Arnold Schoenberg: Five Orchestral Pieces, No. 1 (Premonitions)

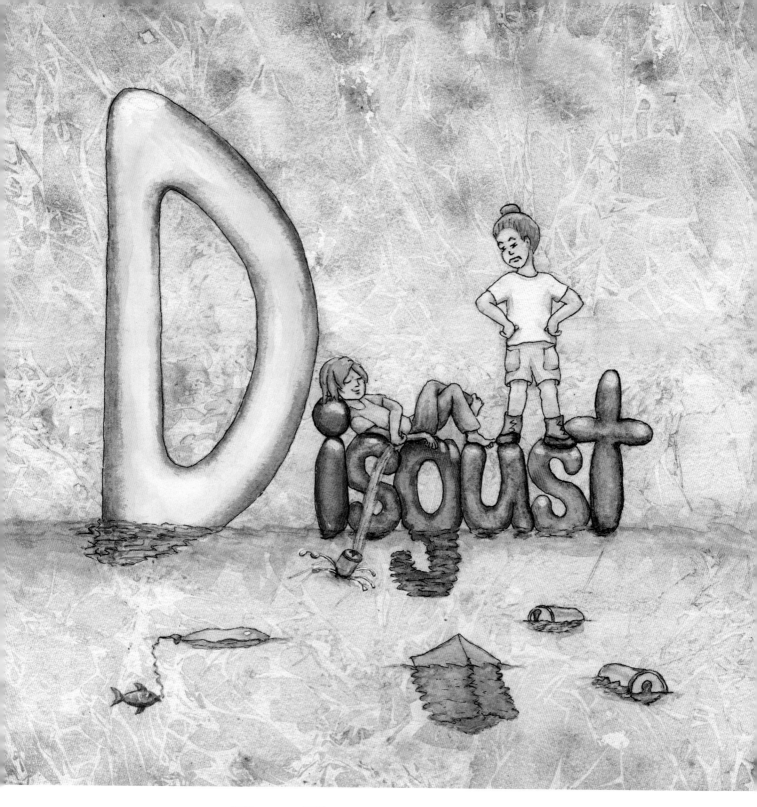

D: Disgust

Franz Liszt: Totentanz

Igor Stravinsky: Sacrificial Dance *from* The Rite of Spring

Ralph Vaughan Williams: Symphony No. 4, mvt. 4 (*Allegro molto*)

E: Excited

John Adams: Short Ride in a Fast Machine

Jacques Offenbach: Overture to Orpheus in the Underworld

Bedřich Smetana: Overture to The Bartered Bride

F: Fear

Krzysztof Penderecki: Threnody to the Victims of Hiroshima

Camille Saint-Saëns: Danse Macabre

Igor Stravinsky: Infernal Dance *from* Firebird Suite

G: Grumpy

Ludwig van Beethoven: Coriolan Overture

Carl Orff: O Fortuna *from* Carmina Burana

Dmitri Shostakovich: Symphony No. 10, mvt. 2 (*Allegro*)

H: Happy

Aaron Copland: Hoe-Down *from* Rodeo

George Frideric Handel: The Arrival of the Queen of Sheba

Gustav Holst: Jupiter, the Bringer of Jollity *from* The Planets

I: Impatient

Béla Bartók: Concerto for Orchestra, mvt. 4 (*Intermezzo interrotto*)

Aram Khachaturian: Sabre Dance

Nikolai Rimsky-Korsakov: Flight of the Bumblebee

J: Jealous

Hector Berlioz: March to the Scaffold *from* Symphonie Fantastique

Georges Bizet: Habanera *from* Carmen Suite No. 2

Wolfgang Amadeus Mozart: Symphony No. 40 in G minor, mvt. 1 (*Allegro molto*)

K: Kind

Cécile Chaminade: Concertino for Flute and Orchestra

Wolfgang Amadeus Mozart: Piano Sonata No. 16 in C major

Pyotr Tchaikovsky: Waltz of the Flowers *from* The Nutcracker

L: Lonely

Johannes Brahms: String Sextet No. 1, mvt. 2 (*Andante*)

Wolfgang Amadeus Mozart: Lacrimosa *from* Requiem

Maurice Ravel: Pavane pour une infante défunte

M: Mischievous

Claude Debussy: Golliwog's Cakewalk *from* Children's Corner

Charles Gounod: Funeral March of a Marionette

Edvard Grieg: In the Hall of the Mountain King *from* Peer Gynt

N: Nervous

Johann Sebastian Bach: Toccata and Fugue in D minor

Antonio Bazzini: The Dance of the Goblins (*Scherzo fantastique*)

Modest Mussorgsky: Night on Bald Mountain

O: Overwhelmed

Johannes Brahms: Hungarian Dance No. 5

Sergei Prokofiev: Montagues and Capulets *from* Romeo and Juliet (Suite No. 2)

Pyotr Tchaikovsky: Violin Concerto in D major, mvt. 3 (*Finale: Allegro vivacissimo*)

P: Proud

Arturo Márquez: Danzón No. 2

John Philip Sousa: The Stars and Stripes Forever

William Grant Still: Afro-American Symphony, mvt. 3 (*Animato*)

Q: Quiet

Claude Debussy: Clair de Lune

Julia Kent: Gardermoen

Johann Sebastian Bach: Air *from* Orchestral Suite No. 3 in D major

R: Relief

Antonio Vivaldi: Spring *from* The Four Seasons

Ludovico Einaudi: I Giorni

Gustav Mahler: Symphony No. 5, part IV (*Adagietto*)

S: Silly

Ludwig van Beethoven: Rondo a Capriccio in G major, Op. 129 (Rage Over a Lost Penny)

Franz Joseph Haydn: String Quartet in E-flat major, Op. 33, No. 2 (The Joke)

Camille Saint-Saëns: Carnival of the Animals, mvt. 14 (Finale)

T: Thankful

Aaron Copland: Simple Gifts *from* Appalachian Spring

Antonín Dvořák: Symphony No. 9 (From the New World), mvt. 2 (*Largo*)

Edward Elgar: Nimrod *from* Enigma Variations

U: Uncomfortable

John Adams: On the Transmigration of Souls (*begin listening at the 15-minute mark*)

Olivier Messiaen: Quartet for the End of Time, mvt. 1 (Liturgy of Crystal)

Antonio Vivaldi: Winter *from* The Four Seasons

V: Valued

Jean Sibelius: Finlandia, Op. 26 (*begin listening at the 5-minute mark*)

Bedřich Smetana: Vltava (The Moldau River) *from* Má Vlast (My Fatherland)

William Walton: Crown Imperial (Coronation March)

W: Weary

Samuel Barber: Adagio for Strings

Astor Piazzola: Oblivion

Pyotr Tchaikovsky: Swan Lake Suite, Op. 20, Scene

X: anXious

Gustav Holst: Mars, the Bringer of War *from* The Planets

György Sándor Ligeti: Volumina

Giuseppe Verdi: Dies Irae *from* Requiem

Y: Yearn

Tomaso Albinoni: Adagio in G minor

Camille Saint-Saëns: Carnival of the Animals, mvt. 7 (Aquarium)

Ludwig van Beethoven: Symphony No. 7, mvt. 2 (*Allegretto*)

Z: Zen

Frédéric Chopin: Prelude Op. 28, No. 15 (Raindrop)

Arvo Pärt: Spiegel im Spiegel

Max Richter: On the Nature of Daylight

About the Authors and Artist

Scott N. Edgar is Associate Professor of Music, Music Education Chair, and Director of Bands at Lake Forest College. Prior to his work in higher education he taught K-12 instrumental music in Ohio and Michigan. Dr. Edgar is the author of *Music Education and Social Emotional Learning: The Heart of Teaching Music* and is an internationally sought-after clinician on the topic. In addition to clinics, he also teaches graduate courses on Musical Social Emotional Learning at VanderCook College of Music. He is a Conn-Selmer Educational Clinician and VH1 Save the Music Foundation Educational Consultant.

Music and the arts have been a part of **Stephanie Edgar's** life since she joined her first children's choir at the age of eight, and have been a passion of hers ever since. A native of Delafield, Wisconsin, Stephanie received her Bachelor of Arts in Vocal Music from the University of Wisconsin-Whitewater, where she also minored in Arts Administration. She went on to sing in the Jacksonville Symphony Orchestra Chorus (Jacksonville, Florida), where she participated in a commercial recording of Orff's *Carmina Burana*. Stephanie was a five-year member of the University Musical Society Choral Union (Ann Arbor, Michigan) where she performed with the Detroit Symphony Orchestra as well as the visiting San Francisco Symphony. After relocating to the Chicago area, where she currently resides with her husband, Scott, and son, Nathan, Stephanie was a member of the Chicago-based Peregrine Vocal Ensemble. Stephanie works as Coordinator of the Center for Academic Success at Lake Forest College in Illinois.

Nancy Sosna Bohm is a retired academic librarian and still-practicing, life-long artist with experience in a variety of media, styles, and subjects. This is her first published illustration project. Nancy studied art as a child at the Suburban Fine Art Center of Highland Park, Illinois, as a teen at the Chicago Art Institute, and later majored in art at the University of Illinois. Decades later she studied under the late watercolorist, Jan Sousa, of Mt. Shasta, California. After Nancy read every book in the children's section of the local library to her young children, she made up original bedtime stories for them on themes of social emotional growth. Nancy made instructional stick puppets and taught printing, handwriting, and drawing to homeschoolers. In illustrating *The ABCs My Feelings and Music*, these skills and experiences have culminated in a single project.